pocket.watch

RYAN'S WORLD™

OFFICIAL

ULTIMATE GUIDE!

Hi! It's **Ryan** from

RYAN
TOYS REVIEW ®

EGMONT

We bring stories to life

First published in Great Britain in 2019 by Egmont UK Limited
The Yellow Building, 1 Nicholas Road, London, W11 4AN

Partial content is taken from *Watch This Book*, published 2018
by Simon Spotlight, an imprint of Simon & Schuster Children's Publishing Division
1230 Avenue of the Americas, New York, New York 10020

ISBN 978 1 4052 9538 3
70638/001
Printed in Italy

ONLINE SAFETY FOR YOUNGER FANS

Spending time online is great fun! Here are a few simple rules to help younger
fans stay safe and keep the internet a great place to spend time.

- Never give out your real name – don't use it as your username
- Never give out any of your personal details
- Never tell anybody which school you go to or how old you are
- Never tell anybody your password except a parent or a guardian
- Be aware that you must be 13 or over to create an account on many sites. Always
check the site policy and ask a parent or a guardian for permission before registering
- Always tell a parent or guardian if something is worrying you

Stay safe online. Any website addresses listed in this book are correct at the time
of going to print. However, Egmont is not responsible for content hosted by third parties.
Please be aware that online content can be subject to change and websites
can contain content that is unsuitable for children. We advise that all
children are supervised when using the internet.

Hi! I'm Ryan!

You might know me from my YouTube channel Ryan ToysReview. I review toys like LEGO, monster trucks and more. I also like to test out science experiments and play video games. My mummy, daddy and twin sisters star in my videos too.

If I had to pick one word to describe myself, it would be "**curious.**" I always ask a lot of questions. My parents say that I'm very outgoing and sociable and that I'm a caring brother to my little sisters.

Age: 7
Height: 1.09m
(3½ feet)
Hair colour:
Dark brown
Eye colour:
Dark brown

My Favourite ....

Ice cream flavour: vanilla

Foods: pizza and oranges

Subjects: maths and music

Sports: football and tennis

Animals: pandas and dinosaurs

Books: Little Critter series

Holiday: Christmas

Season: summer

Colours: neon green and neon blue

Drink: milk

Number: infinity

Emoji: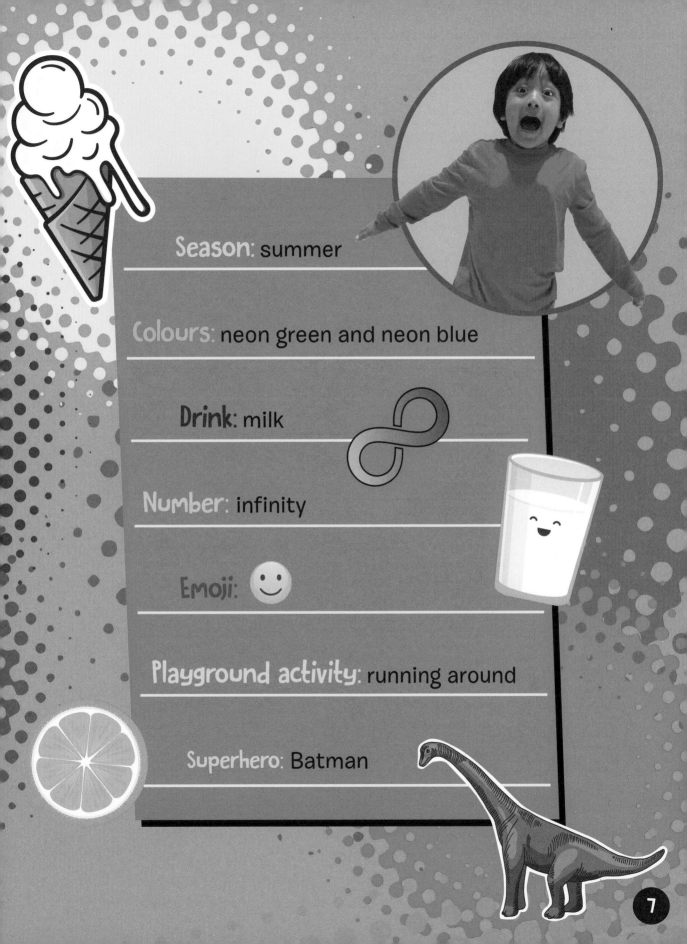

Playground activity: running around

Superhero: Batman

Watch Me!

How I Got Started

When I was three years old, I loved watching other people on YouTube. One day I asked my mummy if we could have our own channel. She said **yes**! We did it just for fun. My first video was about a LEGO train. I liked making the video, so we kept making more. We never ran out of ideas of what to film. We just made videos about things I liked.

Since then, my parents, my sisters and I have uploaded about **one thousand** videos! Now they're about more than just toys. We do skits, challenges, animation, science experiments, gaming and more. The videos are still just as fun to make.

Q: When do you make your videos?

A: We usually film over the weekend during my sisters' naptimes. Each episode usually takes thirty minutes to film.

What It's Really Like to Be on YouTube

It's really exciting to be on YouTube. I love when kids tell me they like my videos. When I got one million subscribers, YouTube gave me a trophy called the **Gold Play Button**. Because I have more than ten million subscribers now, I will get a **Diamond Play Button** award soon.

In every video, we make sure to say goodbye and thank our fans for watching – and we always make sure that we're all having fun playing together. We laugh a lot in our videos.

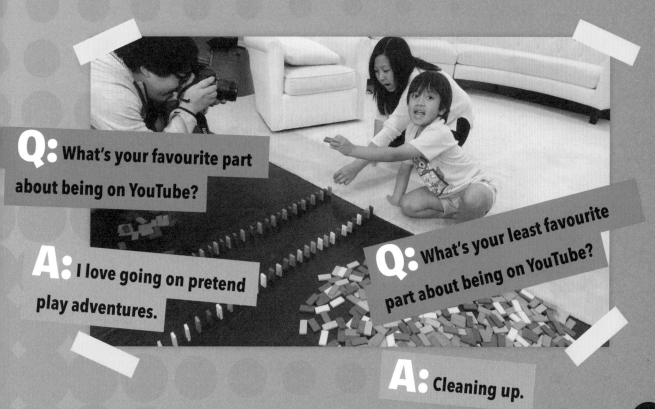

Q: What's your favourite part about being on YouTube?

A: I love going on pretend play adventures.

Q: What's your least favourite part about being on YouTube?

A: Cleaning up.

Inside Ryan ToysReview

SUBSCRIBERS: 18 million+ and climbing!

UPLOADING SINCE: March 2015

TOTAL VIEWS: 23.4 billion+

OTHER CHANNELS: Ryan's Family Review, VTubers, Combo Panda, Gus the Gummy Gator, the Studio Space

My Most-Watched Video

We got more than one billion views on a "Huge Eggs Surprise Toys Challenge" video. I had to climb around a huge inflatable water slide and collect giant colourful eggs. The slide was much bigger than me – even taller than my parents! We set it up in our backyard. It looked like a playground. It had a climbing wall, a fort and a long slide with a sprinkler that ended in a pool of water. The eggs were hidden everywhere! Once I collected them all, I was finally allowed to crack them open. There were toy cars and action figures inside.

Q: What do you do if a video doesn't work out the way you expected?

A: If it's still fun to watch, we call it an epic fail video. Maybe other people can learn from our mistakes!

My Longest Video to Film

The longest time it ever took to film a video was an hour and a half, because we were trying to make a giant chocolate egg and it kept cracking! When you make chocolate eggs, you have to let them harden in a mould. But then removing them from the mould can be really tricky! It's easy for them to break.

Q: What do you think about millions of people watching you?

A: That's a lot of people!

Q: What inspires you?

A: Watching other kids have fun, and having fun with my family.

I Love My Fans!

A lot of people watch my YouTube videos. That means people might recognise me when I leave the house – people I don't even know yet!

I don't mind, though. My fans are always super nice and friendly when I see them in real life. They usually want to tell me that they watch my videos on YouTube. They feel like I'm already their friend! It's cool.

I always have a lot in common with the kids I meet. But I bet you have a lot in common with other kids too!

Q: What does it feel like when someone recognises you?

A: I like it when kids recognise me at the playground because they want to play with me right away and I have a new friend.

Q: What's the one question you always get asked by your fans?

A: How did you get started filming?

How to Make a New Friend

According to Ryan!

1. Say hi!
Don't be shy. Just walk up and say hi to a kid in the playground or at school.

2. Introduce yourself.
Tell them your name and how old you are. Ask them what their name is.

3. Invite them to play with you.
Ask if they'd like to play a game with you or join you in the playground.

4. Ask what they like.
You might find that you have a favourite toy, TV show, or video game in common.

Q: What's the craziest thing you've ever been asked by a fan?

A: "How are you here? I saw you on my iPad!"

SEE, IT'S EASY AND FUN TO MAKE A NEW FRIEND!

A Day in My Life

Mon	Tue	Wed	Thu	Fri	Sat	Sun

Good morning!

On weekdays, my mummy wakes me up for school. I brush my teeth and brush my hair. Sometimes I just make my hair messier, so Mummy helps me.

Then I change into my clothes. Decisions, decisions!

I eat breakfast in the kitchen – usually cereal with milk.

7:00 a.m. *Good Morning!*

MY SISTERS!

Then I say good morning to my **sisters**. I have twin sisters named **Emma** and **Kate**. Some people think they look the same, but I can always tell them apart. Their birthday is in the summer and they just turned three years old. I play with them all the time. We love to play chase and hide-and-seek.

If I had to use one word to describe my twin sisters, it would be "**energetic.**" They really like watching and dancing to nursery rhyme videos.

My Sisters' Favourite . . .

Food:
chopped grapes

Playground activities:
slide and
playing chase

Drink:
milk . . .
just like me!

Ice cream flavour:
vanilla . . .
just like me!

Hobbies:
playing and drawing

Animal:
cat

Mummy!

Daddy!

I also say *good morning* to my **mummy** and **daddy**. Before we made YouTube videos together, my mummy was a high school chemistry teacher and my daddy was a structural engineer. Chemistry is a type of science where people study the matter that makes up our world. A structural engineer helps to build things like buildings and bridges. Cool, right?

I've had no acting experience whatsoever. But I'm not nervous. I'm just filming at home so I'm in my natural setting. I just have fun!

I'm very shy in front of the camera, but Ryan always helps me act funny in the videos.

HEY, PARENTS!

Want to make YouTube videos with your kids?
Ryan's mum and dad have advice.

🔊 Do what the kids enjoy.

We started making LEGO and Thomas & Friends videos because that's what Ryan liked. Now we still play with some toys, but we do more skits and gaming videos. We try to evolve the channel with Ryan's interests.

🔊 Start with a low budget.

Film with your phone, cheap lights and a cheap background. Grow the budget as you grow the channel.

🔊 Be authentic.

It's all about the connection. A lot of kids tell us that when they watch Ryan's videos, they feel like they are watching their friend.

Q&A WITH RYAN'S MUM AND DAD!

Q: What do you want to be doing five years from now?

A: Making fun animation for kids.

Q: What do you like to watch on YouTube (besides your own channel)?

A: News and educational videos about humans and animals.

8:00 a.m. *Time for School!*

Next I put on my shoes and grab my backpack. My mummy drives me to **school**.

The best part of the school day is maths class.

I usually buy my **lunch**. I like eating ice cream sandwiches, milk, Goldfish biscuits, ketchup sandwiches and string cheese.

I also love **pizza**. One day, me and daddy did a fun pizza topping challenge. Mummy filled eggs with secret toppings, and we took turns to open them. I could choose to keep the topping and put it on my pizza or put it on daddy's.

First, I opened an egg and found seaweed. I love seaweed but I don't think it goes well with pizza! Daddy put his Goldfish biscuits on my pizza – my **favourite!**

It was really funny putting yoghurt and chocolate on Daddy's pizza! I didn't like it when he put baked beans on mine.

When all the eggs were open, we put the pizzas in the oven, and each had a slice. **Delicious!**

1:00 p.m. *Science Class!*

After lunch I have **science class**. We learn about how volcanoes erupt.

A volcano is a hill or a mountain on the earth's crust that's connected to a magma chamber underground.

Magma is the name for liquid rock before it reaches the earth's surface. Once it reaches the surface, it's called **lava**!

Volcanoes erupt because of pressure in the earth's surface. Sometimes there is too much pressure and it just **explodes**!

Active volcanoes could erupt at any moment. Dormant volcanoes haven't erupted for more than two hundred years, but they still could erupt in the future. Extinct volcanoes will never erupt again. There are scientists who study volcanoes so we know if they are about to erupt.

It's like when you shake a soda can – the pressure builds until you open it. Then it releases with a ton of fizzy bubbles! The pressure pushes the **magma** up from underground and then it spills onto the earth's surface – now it's **lava**! Lava is a hot liquid that will harden once it's cooled.

Did you know that the Hawaiian Islands were made from volcanoes?

Hawaii

1:30 p.m. *Recess!*

At school, sometimes we get extra recess. Awesome! My friends and I play a game of **Cool or Drool**. Play it with me! After each item, just tell me if you think it's "cool," which means you like it, or "drool," which means you're not that into it.

HERE ARE MY ANSWERS!

Rainbows .... cool

Video games .... cool

Hedgehogs .... cool

Unicorns .... cool

Balloons .... cool

Snow .... cool

The beach .... cool

Candy corn .... cool

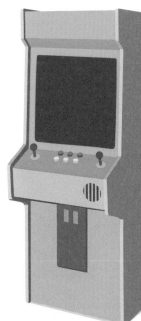

Knock-knock jokes .... cool

Pirates .... cool

Scary stories .... drool

Slime .... cool

Boogers .... drool

Stickers .... cool

Sleepovers .... cool

Pizza .... cool

Bugs .... cool

Dinosaurs .... cool

Baths .... cool

2:00 p.m. Geography Class!

Today we also have geography class. There are so many different places in the world! Some of my **favourite** places are . . .

Disney World

The first ride I rode at Disney World was Splash Mountain, which is a log ride that ends in a big drop with a big splash. When we were waiting in line, a sign said, **YOU MAY GET WET**. We weren't even wearing pool clothes! But Mummy and I decided to try it anyway.

Once we got into the log, we climbed so high. I knew we were going to get so wet! At first there was just a little drop. We didn't get wet at all. But then we kept going. We were almost there! It was finally time for the big drop - **whoosh!** We got wet! It was really fun. I wasn't even scared.

The next time we rode Splash Mountain, Mummy made me hold her hand as we went down the big drop! It was a ton of fun again.

Legoland

Legoland is a theme park filled with LEGO! Building LEGO is one of my favourite things ever. One of my favourite parts of Legoland is the hotel! It's filled with LEGO. They even have **floating LEGO** in the pool. You can build things that float!

We stayed in an Adventure-themed room with a LEGO monkey, spider and scorpion. There were also tons of LEGO to play with in our room, and a scavenger hunt. Besides a big bed for Mummy and Daddy, there were two bunk beds that I got to choose from. Five beds for only three people!

The restaurant had LEGO builds that looked good enough to eat. I wanted to eat the ice cream made from LEGO, but instead I got myself some real ice cream. Mummy told me I had to eat dinner first, though.

Japan

Daddy surprised Mummy and me with a trip to Japan! There are a lot of fun places for kids there, like Universal Studios Japan and a train museum called the Railway Museum. They also have really, really fast trains. They go so fast, they are called bullet trains. In Japanese, they're called *shinkansen*. **I love trains!**

4:00 p.m. *Music Time!*

After school, I go to **music class**. We play songs and there are lots of instruments we can try, like the **drums**, **guitar**, **keyboard**, **shakers** and more. Playing the guitar is fun. I also like playing the drums.

In music class, sometimes the guitar and piano have colours on them, which makes them easier to play. I like music a lot. Fast music is my favourite.

Song videos are one of my favourite kinds of YouTube videos to make. The body parts video was a fun one! It teaches kids the names of the body parts. My sisters like it too. They're in the video clapping. They look so cute. It's hard not to dance when you hear the song.

5:00 p.m. *I'm Home!*

After music class, I go home and do some **chores**. I don't get an allowance, but I help clean up the house once a week.

I **wipe up** the dining room table and living room table with a cleaning spray and paper towels.

Then I bring all my **toys** upstairs. Sometimes I put them in a bag first so they're easier to carry.

Next we sanitise the baby toys by putting them in a little machine for ten minutes.

I put all my Nintendo **games** and my LEGO back where they belong.

I help **vacuum** the rug and furniture with a small, handheld vacuum.

Finally, I help load the dishwasher and the washing machine.

Phew! All done!

What kind of chores do you do to help your family?

Now It's . . .
Family Time!

I love my family!

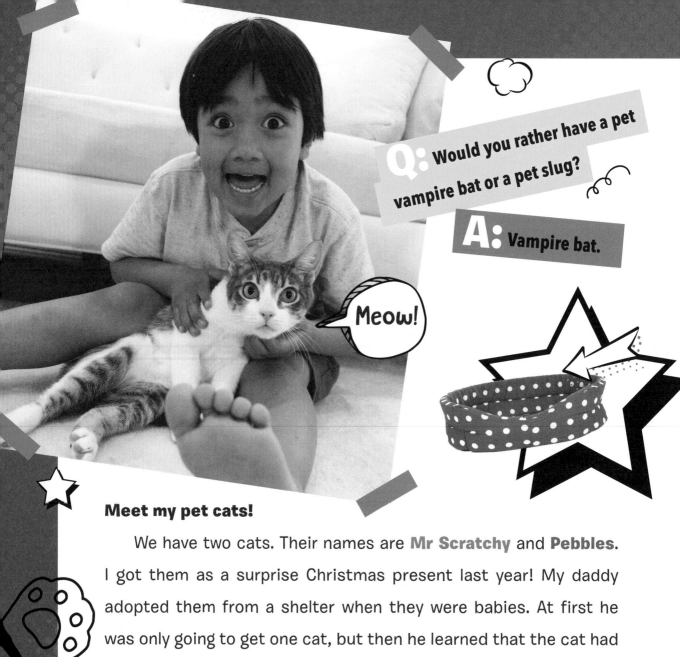

Q: Would you rather have a pet vampire bat or a pet slug?

A: Vampire bat.

Meow!

Meet my pet cats!

We have two cats. Their names are **Mr Scratchy** and **Pebbles**. I got them as a surprise Christmas present last year! My daddy adopted them from a shelter when they were babies. At first he was only going to get one cat, but then he learned that the cat had a brother. So we got two cats! They are about two years old.

Mr Scratchy is a dark grey cat, and Pebbles is light grey with a white belly and paws.

At first the cats were a little scared. Everything in our house was new to them – including me and my sisters! But then the cats started playing with the **toys** we got them. Mr Scratchy was more

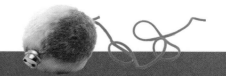

Pebbles

Mr. Scratchy

outgoing. Pebbles was a little bit shy. But before we knew it, they were purring and happy and sitting on my lap!

Once we had pet cats, we needed a few supplies. We went to the pet store and picked out furry **beds** for them. Cats don't need blankets because they have fur.

We also picked up kitty **litter boxes** and a **scratching post** they can climb.

Now that the cats feel comfortable in our home, they are always fighting each other on the floor – it's like they're playing warriors or soldiers or something.

Pebbles likes to look out the window. Sometimes Mr Scratchy will bother him because he wants to play instead.

My sisters also like playing with our pet cats a lot! When we first got them, my sisters were so excited. They thought the cats were so cute that they **screamed**.

6:00 p.m. *Drawing Time!*

It might seem like I'm making videos all the time, but really it's a small part of my life. When I'm not making YouTube videos, I'm reading, **drawing**, playing with LEGO, playing video games or doing puzzles.

Look at this picture I drew!

6:30 p.m. *Dinnertime!*

I love eating dinner with my family. We talk about our days. Tonight my parents and sisters have **a few questions** for me:

Q: What do you want to be when you grow up?

Q: If you could have a superpower, what would it be?

42

Q: If you could invite a famous person on your show, who would it be?

A: I love gaming and would love to meet EthanGamer.

A: A game developer.

A: Flying.

It's almost time to get ready for bed. But first let's play a game of **Would You Rather**! My answers are highlighted in yellow below. What about you? What would you pick?

Would you rather . . .

tell the truth ↖or↗ do a dare?

swim in a pool ↖or↗ swim in the ocean?

live on the moon ↖or↗ live under the sea?

be able to read minds ↖or↗ have X-ray vision?

go back in time ↖or↗ go into the future?

stand forever ↖or↗ sit forever?

eat ice cream ↖or↗ eat candy
for every meal for every meal?

eat all your vegetables ↖or↗ take a bath
every day every day?

stay up late ↖or↗ get up early?

have hair that sticks ↖or↗ have no hair at all?
up all the time

WAKE UP!

Sometimes It's Just Silly Time!

When Is It Filming Time?

You might be wondering when I film my videos. I don't film every day. I usually make my videos over the weekend, during my sisters' naptimes. I make all kinds of **videos**! I've reviewed a lot of toys on my channel, but some of my favourite ones to play with are Spider-Man and Batman **action figures**. I also love LEGO, of course! I watch other people's videos on YouTube too. My favourite videos to watch are EthanGamer, EvanTubeHD and *Roblox* gaming videos.

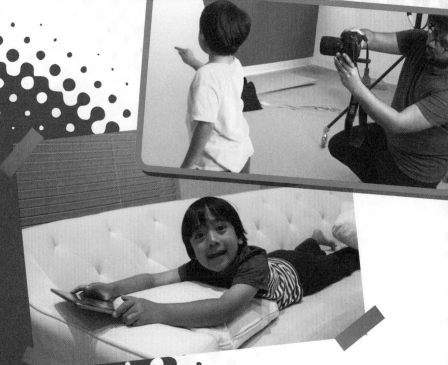

I love my iPad, but my parents limit my screen time. I have thirty minutes on weekdays and one hour on Saturdays and Sundays.

Because my family and I like gaming so much, we actually have a special **gaming room** where we play and film our videos. In our gaming room we have a giant computer, gaming systems like Wii U and PlayStation 4, a giant TV, lots of **games** and of course **cameras**.

We also have lights and a green screen, which lets us change the background of our videos really easily. That's how we make it look like we've **teleported** to a different location. It's all virtual!

I love gaming!

Meet the VTubers!

I have a gaming channel called **VTubers**!

On my channel, we review video games of all kinds.

The *V* in VTubers stands for **"virtual."** When something is virtual, it means it's simulated on a computer – **it's not real**! I collaborate with fun, virtual characters on this channel.

In my first episode of VTubers, I played hide-and-seek on *Roblox* with Combo Panda. I love making dual gaming videos, where you can watch two people playing the same game together.

In my next episode, I played *Kirby Star Allies* with Daddy. We finished the demo version. The game wasn't even out yet!

I can transform into the superstrong and superfast hero **Red Titan!** He can lift weights and can kick through walls. Kapow!

Combo Panda is a hardcore gamer and leader of the combo crew.

Gus the Gator loves yummy gummy sweets and going on crazy adventures. Some people say he make mistakes and do silly things, but he thinks he has a lot of fun!

Moe is from a planet very far away called Moetopia. He likes to be on Earth , eating pizza and building toys. He sometimes gets into trouble, but he always finds a way to get out of it.

Peck the Penguin is from the South Pole. He loves popsicles and one day he hopes to be a great scientist. He loves to study!

Big Gil plays games from his underwater room. He loves Roblox and Mario Kart, where he prefers to be Luigi instead of Mario. He is never afraid to show off his "gil skills".

Alpha Lex is a great gamer with a passion for fashion. She'll stop at nothing to win a game!

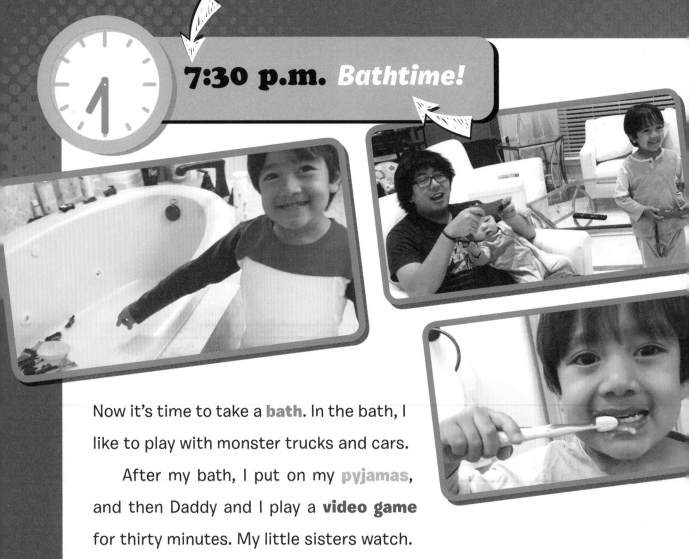

7:30 p.m. *Bathtime!*

Now it's time to take a **bath**. In the bath, I like to play with monster trucks and cars.

After my bath, I put on my **pyjamas**, and then Daddy and I play a **video game** for thirty minutes. My little sisters watch.

Sometimes, before bed, I drink some medicine because I have seasonal allergies and take my **vitamin** gummies.

Then it's time to **brush my teeth**!

Before bed, I play a **board game** or a **card game** with Mummy. Sometimes one of my sisters will play with us if she hasn't fallen asleep yet.

Finally, at about eight thirty p.m., we pick out a **book** to read.

Today was an awesome day!

But

if I could spend a day doing whatever I wanted, I would ...

Eat French fries all day.

Watch my favourite YouTubers.

Drink milk – it's my favourite type of drink!

Build LEGO.

Play Roblox.

Milk

What would you do if you could spend a day doing whatever you wanted?

9:00 p.m. *Bedtime!*

I'm getting sleepy . . .
I can tell because I'm yawning!

Do you know why you yawn?

Your brain is like a computer. When it works hard, it warms up. Playing video games, being active and thinking is hard work for your brain. Your brain needs a break every so often.

You yawn because your brain needs to cool off. When you yawn, you can breathe in more air. That air helps your brain cool down. And that's why you yawn!

Yawning really is contagious. That means if you see someone yawn, it might make you yawn too.

Are you yawning yet?

Yawning isn't just for humans. Animals yawn too. Cats, dogs, snakes, fish – they all yawn.

Now it's time for bed.

I wonder what I'll dream about tonight. Maybe it'll be a peek into my future?

Maybe I'll dream about when I'm twelve years old, and I'm making **gaming videos** for my gaming channel on YouTube. We just started it, and I'd like to grow the channel even more! There are so many video games out there that I'd like to play.

Maybe I'll dream about when I'm twenty-two years old and I'm a **video editor**. That's someone who makes cool videos. I am inspired by the cool animation and virtual stuff that my family makes today. It would be fun to still make videos as an adult!

Goodnight!

Thanks for following me through my day.

See you again on my channel for more fun!

How well do you know Ryan?
Take the ULTIMATE
Ryan's World Quiz.

Ultimate Quiz

The ULTIMATE Ryan's World Quiz!

How well do you know Ryan? Take this quiz to find out!

1. How would Ryan describe himself?
   a. quiet
   b. shy
   c. curious

2. What is Ryan's favourite drink?
   a. milk
   b. orange juice
   c. water

3. How old was Ryan when he made his first YouTube video?
   a. three years old
   b. six years old
   c. ten years old

4. What are Ryan's sisters' names?
   a. Evan and Jillian
   b. Emma and Kate
   c. Jillian and Kate

5. What was Ryan's mum's job before making YouTube videos?
   a. chemistry teacher
   b. actress
   c. professional swimmer

6. What is Ryan's favourite school subject?
   a. maths
   b. gym
   c. none – Ryan doesn't go to school!

7. Ryan's dad surprised Ryan with a trip to which country?
   a. Australia
   b. France
   c. Japan

Quiz continues on p. 63 ...

8. How many cats does Ryan have?
   a. two hundred!
   b. twenty
   c. two

9. What does Ryan want to be when he grows up?
   a. singer
   b. game developer
   c. astronaut

10. BONUS CHALLENGE QUESTION: Which toy has Ryan actually reviewed on his channel?
   a. Lightning McQueen Power Wheels ride-on car
   b. invisible glittery slime
   c. inflatable underwater trampoline

See below to check your answers!

If you got 0-2 questions correct . . . try again!
Are you sure you read this book?

If you got 3-5 questions correct . . . you're a subscriber!
Good job, but you can do even better! Keep watching!

If you got 6-9 questions correct . . . you're a mega-fan!
Wow, your knowledge of Ryan ToysReview is impressive!

If you got 10 questions correct . . . ARE YOU RYAN??
You got all the questions right! How did you do that?

Are you possibly . . .
RYAN HIMSELF??

Answers: 1.c, 2.a, 3.a, 4.b, 5.a, 6.a, 7.c, 8.c, 9.b, 10.a